I SPY
UP IN THE SKY

THE MOON

BY

TAMRA ORR

Mitchell Lane
PUBLISHERS

P.O. Box 196
Hockessin, Delaware 19707
Visit us on the web: www.mitchelllane.com
Comments? email us:
mitchelllane@mitchelllane.com

The Clouds
The Moon
The Stars
The Sun

Printing   1   2   3   4   5   6   7   8   9

ABOUT THE AUTHOR: Award-winning children's book author Tamra Orr lives with her family in the Pacific Northwest.

Library of Congress Cataloging-in-Publication Data
Orr, Tamra.
I spy up in the sky the moon / By Tamra Orr.
    p. cm. — (Randy's corner: I spy up in the sky)
Includes bibliographical references and index.
ISBN 978-1-58415-973-5 (library bound)
1. Moon—Juvenile literature. I. Title.
QB582.O78 2011
523.3—dc22
                                                                      2011000726

eBook ISBN: 9781612281438

                                                                      PLB

I SPY
UP IN THE SKY

THE
MOON

Look up at the night sky.
What can you see?
A big, bright white Moon
Between clouds and trees?

It's as old as Earth,
Made long, long ago,
Reflecting the Sun's light,
Setting darkness aglow.

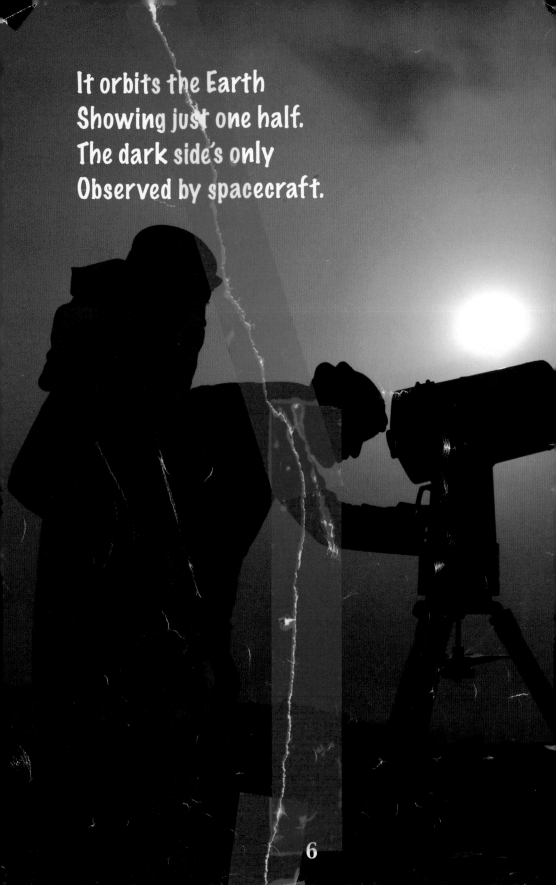

It orbits the Earth
Showing just one half.
The dark side's only
Observed by spacecraft.

Not a real planet,
It's a satellite
That seems to change shape
Almost overnight.

Full Moon

Waxing Gibbous

Last Quarter

The Moon's shape stays the same—
but shadows cause a change.
It all depends on how Earth,
Moon, and Sun are arranged.

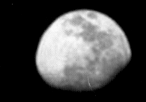

Waning Gibbous

First Quarter

Waxing Crescent

New Moon

The Moon has its phases—
That's how it's designed.
A new moon arises
When Earth blocks sunshine.

As Earth and Sun move,
Less light hits the Moon.
Half becomes a sliver
And then, very soon

The next phase is here.
The new moon is between
The Sun and the Earth,
So it cannot be seen.

Have you ever spotted
A Moon orange-red,
Called the Harvest Moon
Looming up overhead?

The colors come from
Particles in the sky,
And the Moon seems larger
When not up so high.

Wait! What is that
In the bright afternoon?
How is it possible
To see the white Moon?

Even in daytime
The Moon can be spied
As sunrays hit it
And light up its outside.

A ring surrounds the Moon
Reflecting its light
Making a lunar halo
In the middle of the night.

The moonlight shines through
A cloud's crystals of ice
At a twenty-two-degree
Angle—to be precise.

Every now and then,
When Earth, Moon, and Sun
All fall into line,
Watch for some fun!

Earth goes between the
Full Moon and Sun's rays.
A lunar eclipse
Is soon underway.

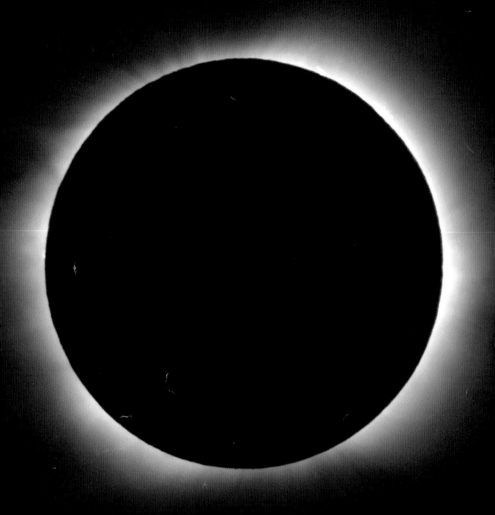

Waves roll in, then glide out
The Moon's sea duty
Pulls them by gravity,
Part of nature's beauty.

Twice a day, there's high tide
And twice a day, low.
Waves pulled onto the shore
And then back out they go.

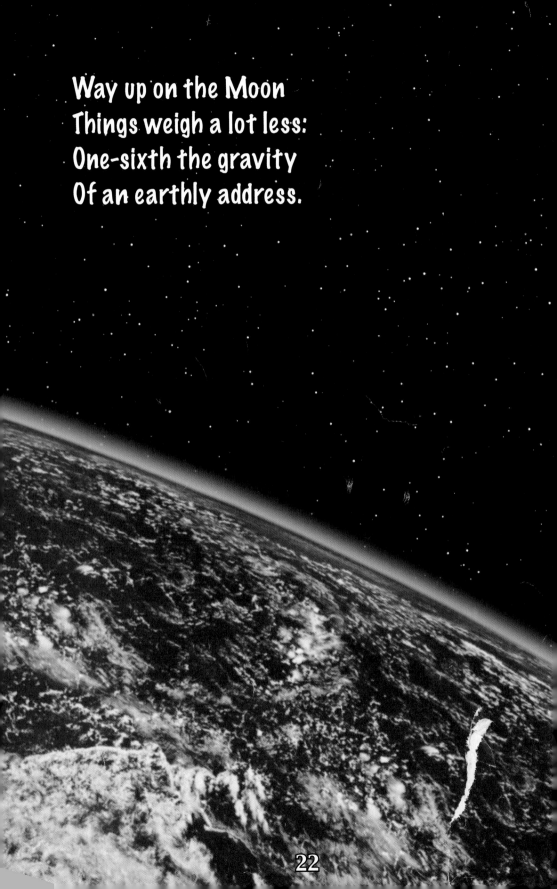

Way up on the Moon
Things weigh a lot less:
One-sixth the gravity
Of an earthly address.

Daylight hours bring heat,
Hundreds of degrees.
Nighttime brings darkness
And a deep, deep freeze.

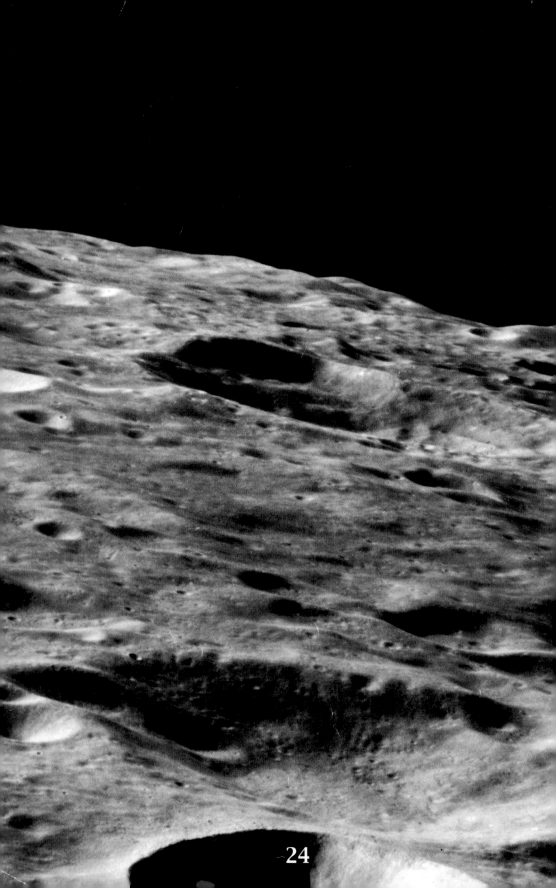

24

On the Moon's surface
Are scars deep and wide
Impacts from comets
Striking its sides.

These trenches are long—
Miles across—and shallow.
The Man in the Moon
Is made by their shadows.

The mysterious Moon
Is an explorer's delight,
Fueling questions
And astronaut flights.

Rocket ships land on
A stark, rocky place,
With mountains and valleys
Across the Moon's face.

So, gaze up at the Moon
And look for the scars.
Imagine you are flying
Among all those stars.

Whether a full moon or new,
Hung low or up high,
The Moon is a beautiful
Part of our sky!

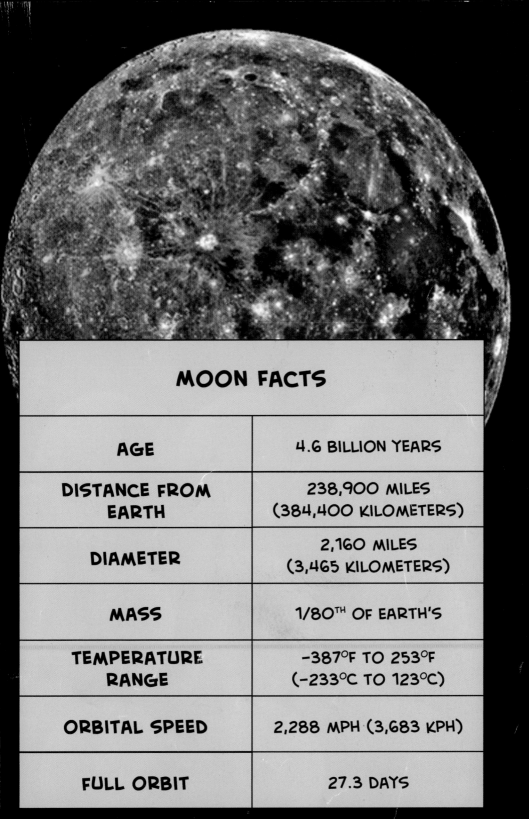

MOON FACTS

AGE	4.6 BILLION YEARS
DISTANCE FROM EARTH	238,900 MILES (384,400 KILOMETERS)
DIAMETER	2,160 MILES (3,465 KILOMETERS)
MASS	1/80TH OF EARTH'S
TEMPERATURE RANGE	-387°F TO 253°F (-233°C TO 123°C)
ORBITAL SPEED	2,288 MPH (3,683 KPH)
FULL ORBIT	27.3 DAYS

THE MOON GLOWS RED DURING AN ECLIPSE

GLOSSARY

eclipse (ee-KLIPS)—When one object in the sky, such as Earth, makes a shadow on another, such as the Moon.

gravity (GRAA-vih-tee)—The force of attraction between objects, such as between Earth and the Moon.

lunar (LOO-nur)—Having to do with the Moon.

lunar halo (LOO-nur HAY-loh)—A glowing circle of light around the Moon.

orbit (OR-bit)—The path that one planet, satellite, or other object takes around another one.

particle (PAR-tih-kul)—A tiny piece.

phase (FAYZ)—One of the steps in a cycle of steps.

rotation (roh-TAY-shun)—A complete turn about an axis, or center line.

satellite (SAA-tuh-lyt)—A natural or human-made object that orbits a planet or star.

tide (TYD)—The rise and fall of the level of the sea, caused by the pull of the Moon's gravity.

FURTHER READING

Books

Florian, Douglas. *Comets, Stars, the Moon, and Mars: Space Poems and Paintings.* New York: Harcourt Children's Books, 2007.

Koontz, Robin. *Hide and Seek Moon: The Moon Phases.* Mankato, Minn.: First Facts Books, 2011.

Lin, Grace. *Thanking the Moon: Celebrating the Mid-Autumn Moon Festival.* New York: Knopf Books for Young Readers, 2010.

Olson, Gillia. *Phases of the Moon.* Mankato, Minn.: Capstone Press, 2008.

Ziefert, Harriet. *By the Light of the Harvest Moon.* Maplewood, N.J.: Blue Apple Books, 2009.

Works Consulted

"NASA's LRO Exposes Moon's Complex, Turbulent Youth." September 16, 2010. http://www.nasa.gov/mission_pages/LRO/news/turbulent-youth.html

NASA Solar System Exploration: Planets: Earth's Moon. http://solarsystem.jpl.nasa.gov/planets/profile.cfm?Object=Moon

Phillips, Tony. "Watch out for the Super Harvest Moon." *NASA Science: Science News*, September 22, 2010. http://science.nasa.gov/science-news/science-at-nasa/2010/22sep_harvestmoon/

Phillips, Tony. "Watch Out for the Harvest Moon." *NASA Science: Science News*, September 16, 2005. http://science.nasa.gov/science-news/science-at-nasa/2000/ast11sep_2/

On the Internet

Dolasia, Meera. "The Earth and Moon Are Still Young Pups!" July 15, 2010. http://www.dogonews.com/2010/7/15/omg-the-earth-and-moon-are-still-young-pups

Lunar Science for Kids: Moon Questions http://lunarscience.arc.nasa.gov/kids/ask

Moon Facts from National Geographic http://news.nationalgeographic.com/news/2004/07/0714_040714_moonfacts.html

NASA's Image of the Day Gallery http://www.nasa.gov/multimedia/imagegallery/iotd.html

The Space Place: How Long Does Each Phase of the Moon Last? http://spaceplace.nasa.gov/en/kids/phonedrmarc/2004_march.shtml

INDEX

PHOTO CREDITS: Cover—Joe Rasemas; p. 6—AFP/Stringer/Getty Images; p. 10—Sue Flood/Getty Images; p. 14—Adam Jones/Stocktrek Images/Getty Images; p. 16—Getty Images; p. 18—Martin Bennetti/AFP/Getty Images; p. 22—Rob Atkins/Getty Images; p. 28—Jacobs Stock Photography/Getty Images. All other photos—CreativeCommons. Every effort has been made to locate all copyright holders of materials used in this book. Any errors or omissions will be corrected in future editions of the book.